50 *Greatest-Ever* SANDWICHES

50 *Greatest-Ever* SANDWICHES

GREAT IDEAS FOR LUNCHBOXES, TASTY SNACKS, GOURMET WRAPS
AND PARTY PIECES, ALL SHOWN STEP BY STEP IN 300 PHOTOGRAPHS

 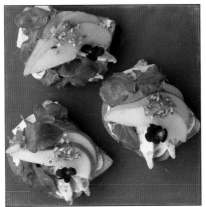 

CAROLE HANDSLIP

LORENZ BOOKS

This edition is published by Lorenz Books, an imprint of Anness Publishing Ltd
Blaby Road, Wigston, Leicestershire LE18 4SE; info@anness.com: www.lorenzbooks.com; www.annesspublishing.com

If you like the images in this book and would like to investigate using them for publishing, promotions or advertising,
please visit our website www.practicalpictures.com for more information.

Publisher: Joanna Lorenz
Editors: Lindsay Porter, Anne Hildyard
Designer: Nigel Partridge
Photographer: Edward Allwright

For all recipes, quantities are given in both metric and imperial measures, and where appropriate, measures are also given in
standard cups and spoons. Follow one set, but not a mixture, because they are not interchangeable. Standard spoon and cup
measures are level. 1 tsp = 5ml, 1 tbsp = 15ml, 1 cup = 250ml/8fl oz. Australian standard tablespoons are 20ml. Australian
readers should use 3 tsp in place of 1 tbsp for measuring small quantities. American pints are 16fl oz/2 cups. American
readers should use 20fl oz/2.5 cups in place of 1 pint when measuring liquids. Electric oven temperatures in this book are for
conventional ovens. When using a fan oven, the temperature will probably need to be reduced by about 10–20°C/20–40°F.
Since ovens vary, you should check with your manufacturer's instruction book for guidance.
Medium (US large) eggs are used unless otherwise stated.

PUBLISHER'S NOTE
Although the advice and information in this book are believed to be accurate and true at the time of going to press,
neither the authors nor the publisher can accept any legal responsibility or liability for any errors or omissions
that may have been made nor for any inaccuracies nor for any loss, harm or injury that comes about from
following instructions or advice in this book.

Contents

Introduction

The sandwich is said to have taken its name from an English Earl. The fourth Earl of Sandwich (1718–92) was such a keen gambler that he did not wish to waste any time eating away from the gaming tables, so he asked a waiter to have cold beef placed between two slices of bread in order to continue playing while he was eating. This very convenient manner of taking sustaining nourishment quickly became popular, and in an acknowledgement to its inventor was forever afterward known as the 'sandwich'.

Below: Cucumber sandwiches are delicious when served at a summer tea party or picnic.

Though the basic idea has remained the same for more than two hundred years, there are now many permutations. The variety and availability of different and excellent breads is enormous, and ideas for fillings abound throughout the world. Each country has its own particular way of preparing this quick and easy snack. In Spain they make *bocadillas*, long rolls stuffed with Serrano ham. In Italy *bruschetta* is a toasted, peasant bread lavishly spread with garlic, olive oil and sometimes tomato. In northern Europe, Germany offers black or rye breads with smoky Westphalia ham. Scandinavia uses pumpernickel with many varieties of herring. From America we have triple-decker club sandwiches and torpedo rolls filled to bursting, called 'heroes', designed to satisfy an heroic appetite! From the East come tikka, satay and other hot, spicy goodies which can be stuffed into pitta bread or simply wrapped in naan – the variety is endless.

In this book are recipes ideal to pack for picnics or to make a lunch box more interesting; there are some super surprises for a children's tea party; and recipes that provide inviting tasty food for the unexpected visitor. When it's too late to prepare a cooked meal, a simple slice of bread with butter will be perfect.

Right: Open sandwiches, such as this one topped with salt beef and avocado, look attractive on a buffet table or just for a light lunch.

Seasonings

Sandwiches are quick and easy, and it is worth maintaining a well-stocked store-cupboard and refrigerator, so that you can rustle up a satisfying snack at a moment's notice.

If you have good bread, and ingredients such as tuna fish, anchovies, olives, rollmops, olive oil, a jar of pesto, olive paste, mayonnaise and sun-dried tomatoes, you will be able to provide a feast. Once opened, bottled sauces should be stored in the refrigerator, where they will keep for a month, but check the labels. Ready-made mustard can be kept in the store-cupboard for a few months.

Dill mustard sauce
This is a sweetish sauce with dill and sour cream. It is served with gravlax.

Extra-virgin olive oil
This oil is used to add taste to marinades and dressings, and as a dip for bread.

Jalapeño peppers
These pickled green chillies are from Mexico; they are very hot, and are a useful addition to tacos and tostados.

Mustards
Made from black, brown or white mustard seeds, spices and vinegar. Mustards with added ingredients include horseradish, honey, chilli and tarragon. Meaux mustard is grainy and spicy and made from mixed mustard seed. Dijon mustard is sharp, and is ideal in dressings, while German mustard is best with frankfurters.

Olive paste
Made with puréed black or green olives, olive oil and herbs, it is delicious on its own, and good spread on bread before covering with topping and grilling (broiling), and for adding to sauces.

Pesto
The green version is a rich, pungent sauce made with basil, Parmesan cheese, pine nuts and garlic. Red pesto is the same, but it is made with sun-dried tomatoes.

Sauerkraut
This salted and fermented white cabbage is good with sausages. Mix with tomato mayonnaise and use in sandwiches.

Sun-dried tomatoes
Preserved whole by drying, they have a dense texture and concentrated taste.

Left: This selection of storecupboard ingredients is useful for sandwiches.

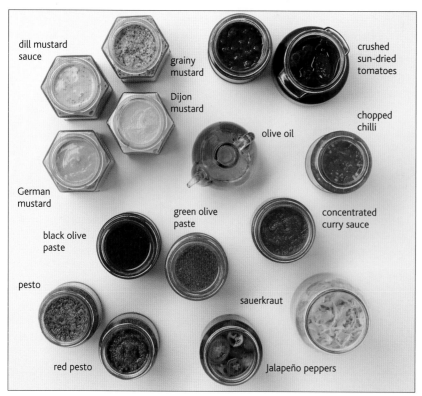

dill mustard sauce

grainy mustard

Dijon mustard

crushed sun-dried tomatoes

chopped chilli

olive oil

German mustard

green olive paste

concentrated curry sauce

black olive paste

pesto

sauerkraut

red pesto

Jalapeño peppers

Herbs and Flowers

Fresh herbs can give terrific zip to a sandwich filling. They can easily be grown, either in the garden or on a windowsill, and have so much more flavour when they are freshly picked.

Edible flowers make a delightful garnish, are pretty and have a sweet taste. Marigolds, pansies, violas, and violets can all be used, as can herb flowers such as borage, thyme, marjoram, mint and rosemary. All add colour and flavour.

Basil
With its warm, spicy scent and pungent aroma, basil is good with tomatoes, and used either cooked in a sauce or as fresh leaves added to a sandwich filling.

Chives
The delicate, mild, onion taste is good in sauces and fillings. The slender leaves make attractive garnishes, and the beautiful purple flowers can also be eaten.

Coriander (Cilantro)
Essential for Indian, Chinese and Mexican dishes owing to its intensely aromatic herb and spicy aroma.

Fennel and Dill
These herbs, from the same family, have feathery leaves, but fennel has a definite aniseed taste. They are good with fish.

Marjoram and Oregano
These herbs belong to the same family , oregano is a little stronger. They are good in tomato sauces and egg dishes.

Mint
Good as a garnish, mixed with soft cheeses, or added to grilled (broiled) meats.

Nasturtium
The flowers are good in sandwiches; the leaves have a peppery quality.

Parsley
Curled and flat-leaf parsley are both available, the latter having the stronger taste. Apart from being an attractive garnish, parsley is also excellent chopped and added to a herb butter.

Above: These herbs all made a good addition to a sandwich filling.

Rocket (arugula)
The peppery, warm taste of rocket makes it a good addition to many fillings.

Thyme
For the best results, thyme should be used in cooked dishes or sauces.

Breads

Bread in different sizes, shapes, textures, tastes, and various shades of brown, can produce exciting and tasty sandwiches.

Bagel
Best served warm, bagels are especially good when filled with cream cheese and smoked salmon or mackerel pâté.

Baguette
Also called French sticks, they are split lengthways, grilled, then sliced for filling.

Brioche
This light, rich, slightly sweet bread makes a good base for open sandwiches when it is toasted.

Ciabatta
Made with olive oil, this bread has a light, airy texture. It is available plain or with garlic.

Cottage loaf
A crusty white loaf, suitable for hearty and toasted sandwiches.

Croissant
Delicious with any type of filling. Warm croissants first, then split and fill them.

Flavoured sticks
These might include granary, onion bread and cheese and herb sticks. They all make excellent sandwiches.

Pitta bread
These are available in both wholemeal and white, in rounds, ovals and mini cocktail shapes. They are ideal for filling with grilled meats and salads.

Pugliese
This is also known as Italian peasant bread, and is a close-textured loaf made with olive oil.

Pumpernickel
This is a heavy, close-textured black rye bread with a distinctive taste. It is excellent as a base for open sandwiches, topped with meats or cheese.

Tortilla
This traditional Mexican pancake comes in corn and wheat varieties. Always warm first before serving with a tasty filling.

Rye bread
Available light and dark; both are delicious with pickled herring.

Rye with sunflower seeds
This is similar to pumpernickel but lighter in tone and taste. It is a good base for open sandwiches.

White bread
This need not be the pre-packaged, pre-sliced variety. Bakeries will make their own varieties, which have a lot more taste and a better texture.

Wholemeal (wholewheat) bread
This bread is preferred by some to white bread for its texture and nutty taste.

Right: A selection of breads, showing the wide choice available.

pitta bread

croissants

pugliese (Italian peasant bread)

bagels

ciabatta

ciabatta rolls

baguette

brioche

half baguette

wheat tortillas

granary stick

rye breads

pumpernickel

corn tortillas

rye bread with sunflower seeds

white loaf

wholemeal (wholewheat) bread

cottage loaf

Cheese and Tomato Bread

This wholesome bread mix, with tomato and Parmesan cheese can be shaped into rolls, sticks, rounds or loaves, then topped with cracked wheat or sesame seeds before baking.

Makes 2 sticks

225 g/8 oz/2 cups wholemeal (wholewheat) flour
225 g/8 oz/2 cups plain (all-purpose) flour
5 ml/1 tsp salt
5 ml/1 tsp dried yeast
300 ml/10 fl oz/1¼ cups warm water
pinch of sugar
30 ml/2 tbsp tomato purée (paste) or
   sun-dried tomato paste
25 g/1 oz/¼ cup grated Parmesan cheese
4 spring onions (scallions), chopped
cracked wheat or sesame seeds

2 Add the tomato purée (paste), cheese, spring onions (scallions) and remaining water. Mix to a soft dough, adding a little more water if necessary.

5 Turn out on to a floured surface and knead again for a few minutes. Divide the dough in half, shape each portion into a stick 30 cm/12 in long and place diagonally on a greased baking-sheet.

1 Mix the flours and salt in a bowl. Put the yeast in a small bowl and mix in half the water and a pinch of sugar. Leave for 10 minutes to dissolve, add to the flour.

GRANARY BREAD

Replace the plain (all-purpose) flour with malted brown flour and omit the last 4 ingredients. Shape the dough into an oblong and place it in a greased 450 g/1 lb loaf tin (bread pan). Bake as above, but allow an extra 5 minutes.

3 Turn out on to a floured surface and knead for 5 minutes until the dough is smooth and elastic.

4 Place in a mixing bowl, cover with a damp cloth and leave in a warm place to rise until doubled in size.

CHEESE AND TOMATO ROLLS

Divide the dough into 8 portions and shape into rolls. Bake for 20–25 minutes.

6 Make diagonal cuts down the length of the sticks, brush with water and sprinkle with cracked wheat or sesame seeds. Cover and leave in a warm place to rise for about 30 minutes until doubled in size. Pre-heat the oven to 220°C/425°F/ gas mark 7. Bake in the oven for 10 minutes, then lower the temperature to 200°C/400°F/gas mark 6 and bake for a further 15 minutes.

Filling Ingredients

As well as fresh bread, the basic elements in a sandwich are usually protein, leafy vegetables and a tasty spread or sauce.

Avocado
This is perfect served with Brie or prawns (shrimp).

Blue cheese
This cheese is a good partner for pears.

Brie
When it is soft in the centre, Brie is delicious with avocado and tomato.

Capers
These add piquancy to dressings.

Cucumber
Remove the skin for sandwich fillings.

Gruyère or Emmenthal (Swiss) cheese
This is the classic cheese for melting under the grill.

Hens' eggs
Use with a variety of toppings.

Lemon
A tasty addition to fish fillings.

Lettuce
Try any variety in sandwiches.

Mozzarella
This cheese blends well with basil, sun-dried tomatoes and olive paste.

Olives
These are a particularly good addition to toasted toppings.

Parma ham
This is cured, matured ham, which is sliced thinly. Use for party sandwiches.

Parmesan
Use freshly grated for the best result.

Pastrami
Pastrami is cured brisket of beef, which is then smoked. Served with rye bread.

Peppers
A crunchy, tasty filling ingredient.

Prawns (shrimp)
For the best taste, use cold-water prawns (shrimp).

Quails' eggs
Use for open sandwiches. Boil for 5 minutes, plunge into cold water and peel.

Rollmop herrings
With other varieties of pickled herring, rollmops are good on open sandwiches.

Salami
Smoked and unsmoked are available.

Smoked salmon
Ideal for open sandwiches and pinwheels.

Tomatoes
Select deep red for sweetness.

Right: Use some of these popular ingredients for tasty sandwich fillings.

Gruyère (Swiss) cheese

blue cheese

Brie cheese

Parmesan cheese

prawns (shrimp)

smoked salmon

pastrami

lemon

avocado

tomatoes

mozzarella

cucumber

lollo rosso
lettuce

salami

rollmop herring

quails' eggs

peppers

hens' eggs

frisée lettuce

olives

Parma ham

Mayonnaise

Mayonnaise can be prepared with a little olive oil to give a rich taste, but the result is heavy if olive oil is used solely. It can be whisked by hand, but may also be made in a food processor or blender.

Makes about 350 ml/12 fl oz/1½ cups

2 egg yolks
salt and pepper
2.5 ml/½ tsp Dijon mustard
300 ml/10 fl oz/1¼ cups sunflower oil
10 ml/2 tsp wine vinegar

1 Beat the egg yolk, seasoning and mustard together in a bowl with a hand whisk. Add the oil drop by drop, whisking vigorously.

COOK'S TIP
Store in an airtight container in the refrigerator for up to 2 weeks.

2 As the mixture thickens, add the vinegar, then continue to add the remaining oil in a steady stream, whisking all the time. Add a little boiling water to thin if necessary.

Gravlax Sauce

This is used with gravlax, Scandinavian marinated salmon, but its piquant taste is a good partner for beef, too. It will keep for up to 2 weeks in a sealed container in the refrigerator.

Makes about 150 ml/5 fl oz/⅔ cup

30 ml/2 tbsp German mustard
5 ml/1 tsp caster (superfine) sugar
5 ml/1 tsp wine vinegar
30 ml/2 tbsp oil
30 ml/2 tbsp sour cream
15 ml/1 tbsp chopped fresh dill

1 Beat the mustard, sugar and vinegar together. Gradually add the oil, beating well between each addition.

COOK'S TIP
The sauce can be served with any smoked or poached fish or seafood.

2 Beat the mixture with a wire whisk until thickened, then whisk in the cream and dill. Season to taste.

Peanut Sauce

This peanut sauce is traditionally served with Indonesian satay, but it is good with chicken, duck or pork and any vegetable filling, in a sandwich. It keeps for up to 1 week in the refrigerator.

Makes about 300 ml/10 fl oz/1¼ cups

15 ml/1 tbsp sunflower oil
1 small onion, chopped
1 garlic clove, crushed
5 ml/1 tsp ground cumin
5 ml/1 tsp ground coriander
2.5 ml/½ tsp chilli powder
45 ml/3 tbsp crunchy peanut butter
10 ml/2 tsp soy sauce
5 ml/1 tsp lemon juice

1 Heat the oil and fry the onion. Add the garlic and spices and fry for a further 1 minute, stirring. Mix in the peanut butter and blend in 150 ml/5 fl oz/⅔ cup water.

2 Bring to the boil, stirring, then cover and cook for 5 minutes. Turn into a bowl and stir in the soy sauce and lemon juice. Thin with a little more water if liked. Allow to cool.

Fennel and Sour Cream Dressing

A light, creamy dressing to use with fish or cucumber fillings. You can make a green herb sauce by adding 45 ml/3 tbsp chopped fresh parsley, chives and mint. It keeps for up to 1 week in the refrigerator.

Makes about 150 ml/5 fl oz/⅔ cup

100 ml/4 fl oz/½ cup thick sour cream
10 ml/2 tsp lemon juice
1 garlic clove, crushed
5 ml/1 tsp clear honey
30 ml/2 tbsp chopped fresh fennel
salt and pepper

1 Put the sour cream into a medium bowl, add the lemon juice, garlic and honey and mix thoroughly.

2 Stir in the chopped fennel and some salt and pepper.

Equipment

Very little equipment is needed, apart from a bread knife so that you can slice bread and cut sandwiches into portions.

Hot sandwich makers are by no means essential for making toasted or fried sandwiches – a frying-pan (skillet) or griddle does just as well. If you want to make sandwiches for special occasions, or add extra garnishes, the following pieces of equipment may be useful.

Bread knife
A good-quality bread knife will ensure bread is cut evenly.

Cheese grater
This is invaluable for preparing fillings, both for grating hard cheeses and vegetables such as carrots.

Cutters
Both plain and shaped cutters are useful for making party sandwiches and canapés. Novelty cutters will appeal especially to children.

Knives
Keep knives clean and well sharpened.

Measuring cups
When using measuring cups and spoons make sure you keep to one system of measurement (i.e. metric, imperial or cups).

Measuring spoons
Accurate measuring spoons are essential to successful baking.

Mixing bowls
A set of mixing bowls of various sizes is invaluable. Keep large bowls on hand for making bread (to allow the dough to rise).

Palette knives
The rounded ends of palette knives are useful for spreading fillings smoothly.

Pastry brush
A pastry brush is useful both for bread and sandwich making. Use for egg glazes on uncooked bread dough, and for brushing bread with melted butter or oils.

Rolling pin
When making sandwiches such as Asparagus Rolls, flatten slices of bread with a heavy rolling pin, so that the slices roll up more easily.

Saucepan
A heavy metal saucepan should be used for melted and cooked fillings.

Spatula
Use a flexible spatula for spreading and transferring fillings from mixing bowls.

Spoons, metal
Ordinary soup and dessert spoons may be used for mixing ingredients.

Spoons, wooden
Wooden spoons may be used for mixing both hot and cold fillings.

Wire whisk
Use a whisk to mix hot fillings and sauces.

mixing bowls

cheese grater

bread knife

palette knives

wire whisk

saucepan

metal spoons

cutters

pastry
brush

wooden
spoon

measuring jug

rolling pin

knives

measuring spoons

spatula

Fillings

These three quick and easy fillings of avocado, tuna and tomato and egg and cress are perfect to fill slices of bread, rolls, croissants or open sandwiches.

AVOCADO FILLING

This filling is particularly suitable for sandwich horns, croissants or on open sandwiches.

1 avocado, stoned (pitted) and chopped
1 spring onion (scallion), chopped
10 ml/2 tsp lemon juice
dash Worcestershire sauce
salt and pepper

1 Put the avocado pieces in a blender, or mash with a fork until smooth. Mix in the chopped spring onion, lemon juice and seasonings and blend well.

TUNA AND TOMATO FILLING

This recipe is sufficient to make 3 rounds of sandwiches.

75 g/3 oz can tuna fish, drained
25 g/1 oz/2 tbsp softened butter or soft white (farmer's) cheese
15 ml/1 tbsp tomato ketchup
15 ml/1 tbsp mayonnaise
salt and pepper

1 Put the tuna fish in a bowl and flake with a fork. Add the butter or soft cheese, tomato ketchup and mayonnaise and season to taste. Mix well until blended.

EGG AND CRESS FILLING

This recipe is sufficient to make 3 rounds of sandwiches.

2 hard-boiled eggs, shelled and finely chopped
50 g/2 oz/¼ cup curd (smooth cottage) cheese
30 ml/2 tbsp mayonnaise
salt and pepper
1 carton mustard and cress

1 Mix all the ingredients together in a bowl until thoroughly combined and smooth.

Garnishes

The presentation of food is almost as important as the taste. If food appears attractive and appetizing, there will be a desire to eat. These garnishes look good, and add texture.

RADISH ROSE

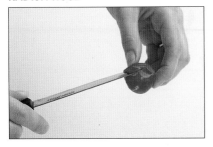

Remove the stalk, and with the pointed end of a vegetable knife cut petal shapes round the bottom half of the radish, keeping them joined at the base. Cut a second row of petals in between and above the first row, and continue in this way until you reach the top of the radish. Leave in iced water for about an hour until it opens.

SPRING ONION (SCALLION) TASSEL

Trim a spring onion to about 7.5 cm/3 in long. Cut lengthways through the green part of the onion several times, to 4 cm/1½ in of the white end. Place in a bowl of iced water, until the ends curl up.

CARROT CURL

Using a potato peeler remove thin strips of carrot. Roll each strip to make a curl and secure with a cocktail stick (toothpick). Place in iced water for about an hour to keep the shape.

CUCUMBER BUTTERFLIES

Cut a 1 cm/½ in length of cucumber and halve lengthways into 2 semi-circles. Cut each into 7 slices, leaving them attached along one edge. Fold every other slice back on itself to form the butterfly.

RADISH CHRYSANTHEMUM

First remove the stalk, then cut downwards across the radish, using a sharp knife, at 2 mm/1/16 in intervals, keeping the radish joined at the base. Then cut in the opposite direction to form minute squares. Drop into iced water for about an hour, until it opens out like a flower.

TOMATO ROSE

Choose a firm tomato and, starting at the smooth end, pare off the skin in a continuous strip about 1 cm/½ in wide using a sharp knife. With the flesh side inwards, start to curl the strip of skin from the base end, forming a bud shape. Continue winding the strip into a flower.

Filled Croissants

Croissants are delicious just as they are, but are even better when they are filled with a tasty mixture, baked then served hot.

Makes 2

2 croissants
knob of butter
2 eggs
salt and pepper
1 tablespoon double (heavy) cream
50 g/2 oz smoked salmon, chopped
1 sprig fresh dill, to garnish

1 Preheat the oven to 180°C/350°F/gas mark 4. Slice the croissants in half horizontally and warm in the oven for 5–6 minutes.

2 Melt a knob of butter. Beat the eggs in a bowl with seasoning to taste.

3 Add the eggs to the pan and cook for 2 minutes, stirring constantly.

4 Remove from the heat and stir in the cream and smoked salmon.

5 Spoon the smoked salmon mixture into the croissants and garnish with dill sprigs.

FETA AND TOMATO FILLING
Fill a croissant with 25g/1 oz feta cheese and 2 chopped sun-dried tomatoes. Bake for 5 minutes as above.

PEAR AND STILTON FILLING
Soften 100 g/4 oz Stilton cheese with a fork and mix in 1 peeled, cored and chopped ripe pear and 15 ml/1 tbsp chives with a little black pepper. Spoon into a split croissant and bake in a preheated oven for 5 minutes.

Crispy Hot Dogs

Crisp little envelopes enclose succulent frankfurters, which are served German-style with sauerkraut. The hot dogs can be varied by using different sauces.

Makes 8

8 slices white or brown bread,
    crusts removed
50 g/2 oz/4tbsp softened butter
15 ml/1 tbsp German mustard
8 frankfurters
sauerkraut, to serve
tomato wedges and flat-leaf parsley,
    to garnish

COOK'S TIP
Instead of frankfurters, use grilled (broiled) sausages if you prefer.

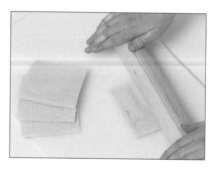

1 Preheat the oven to 200°C/400°F/gas mark 6. Roll the bread lightly with a rolling pin so that it rolls up more easily.

2 Spread the bread with a little butter and mustard.

3 Place a frankfurter diagonally across each slice of bread and roll up tightly, securing with a cocktail stick (toothpick). Spread each roll with margarine and place on a baking sheet. Bake in the oven for 15–20 minutes until golden.

4 Meanwhile heat the sauerkraut. Remove the cocktail sticks from the hot dogs and serve with hot sauerkraut and a garnish of tomato wedges and flat-leaf parsley.

Croque Monsieur

Probably the most popular snack food in France, this tasty, hot cheese and ham sandwich can be served either fried or grilled (broiled).

Makes 2

4 slices white bread
25 g/1 oz/2 tbsp softened butter
2 thin slices lean ham
50 g/2 oz Gruyère (Swiss) cheese,
    thinly sliced
1 sprig flat-leaf parsley, to garnish

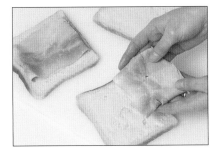

1 Spread the bread with butter. Lay the ham on 2 of the buttered sides of bread.

COOK'S TIP
A tasty butter can be used to complement a sandwich filling – for example, horseradish butter with beef, mustard butter with ham, lemon and dill butter with fish. To make these just beat the chosen ingredient into the softened butter with some seasoning. Other useful flavourings for butter are: anchovy or curry paste, garlic, herbs, Tabasco or chilli. These butters can also be used in open sandwiches.

2 Lay the Gruyère (Swiss) cheese slices on top of the ham and sandwich with the buttered bread slices. Press firmly together and cut off the crusts.

3 Spread the top with butter, place on a rack and cook for 2½ minutes under the grill (broiler) preheated to a low to moderate temperature.

4 Turn the sandwiches over, spread the remaining butter over the top and return to the grill for a further 2½ minutes until the bread is golden brown and the cheese is beginning to melt. Garnish with a sprig of flat-leaf parsley.

Bruschetta al Pomodoro

Bruschetta is an Italian garlic bread made with the best-quality olive oil you can find and pugliese, a coarse country bread, or ciabatta. Here, chopped tomatoes are added too.

Makes 2

2 large thick slices coarse country bread
1 large garlic clove
60 ml/4 tbsp extra-virgin olive oil
2 ripe tomatoes, skinned and chopped
salt and pepper
1 sprig fresh basil, to garnish

1 Toast the bread on both sides.

2 Peel the garlic clove and squash with the flat side of a knife blade.

3 Rub the squashed garlic clove over the toast.

4 Drizzle half the olive oil over the toasted bread.

5 Top with the chopped tomatoes, season well and drizzle over the remaining oil. Place under the grill (broiler) to heat through, then garnish with a sprig of basil and eat immediately.

PLAIN BRUSCHETTA
Rub a crushed garlic clove over untoasted bread, drizzle with oil and then toast.

Pastrami on Rye

Pastrami is wood-smoked brisket of beef that has first been dry-cured in a mixture of garlic, sugar, salt and spices. This is a kosher sandwich that originates from New York.

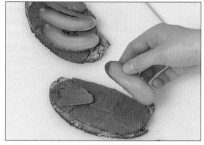

2 Arrange the pastrami slices over the mustard.

Makes 2

25 g/1 oz/2 tbsp softened butter
4 thin slices rye bread
15 ml/1 tbsp German mustard
100 g/4 oz wafer-thin pastrami
4 gherkins (dill pickles), sliced lengthways
radish chrysanthemums and spring onion
    (scallion) tassels, to garnish

1 Butter the bread and spread 2 of the slices with a little mustard.

3 Top with slices of gherkin (dill pickle), cover with the remaining bread and press together firmly. Toast on both sides under a preheated grill (broiler) until turning brown. Serve garnished with radish chrysanthemums and spring onion (scallion) tassels.

COOK'S TIP
Any type of rye bread can be used, from those with a light texture and shade to the very dense, dark pumpernickel.

Fried Mozzarella Sandwich

This sandwich is very popular in southern Italy, where it is known as *Mozzarella in Carrozza*. It is also excellent made with Cheddar or Gruyère (Swiss) cheese.

Makes 2

100 g/4 oz mozzarella cheese,
    thickly sliced
4 thick slices white bread, crusts removed
salt and pepper
1 egg
30 ml/2 tbsp milk
oil for shallow-frying

3 Dip the sandwiches in the egg mixture, turn and leave for a few minutes. Heat 1 cm/½ oil and fry the sandwich for 3–4 minutes, turning once, until golden brown and crisp. Drain well on kitchen paper.

VARIATION

Add 2 chopped sun-dried tomatoes or some black olive paste to the sandwich before soaking in egg.

1 Lay the mozzarella slices on 2 slices of bread, sprinkle with salt and pepper, then top with the remaining bread slices to make 2 cheese sandwiches.

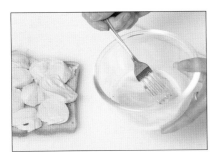

2 Mix the egg and milk together, season and place in a large shallow dish.

Tostadas with Refried Beans

A tostada is a crisp, fried tortilla used as a base on which to pile the topping of your choice – a variation on a sandwich, and a very tasty snack popular in Mexico and South America.

Makes 6

30 ml/2 tbsp oil
1 onion, chopped
2 garlic cloves, chopped
2.5 ml/½ tsp chilli powder
425 g/15 oz can borlotti or pinto
    beans, drained
150 ml/5 fl oz/⅔ cup chicken stock
15 ml/1 tbsp tomato purée (paste)
30 ml/2 tbsp chopped fresh
    coriander (cilantro)
salt and pepper
6 wheat or corn tortillas
45 ml/3 tbsp Tomato Salsa
30 ml/2 tbsp sour cream
50 g/2 oz/½ cup grated Cheddar cheese
fresh coriander (cilantro) leaves,
    to garnish

1 Heat the oil in a pan and fry the onion until softened.

2 Add the garlic and chilli powder and fry for 1 minute, stirring.

3 Mix in the beans and mash very roughly with a potato masher.

4 Add the stock, tomato purée (paste), chopped coriander and seasoning to taste. Mix and cook for a few minutes.

5 Fry the tortillas in hot oil for I minute, turning once, until crisp, then drain on kitchen paper.

6 Put a spoonful of refried beans on each tostada, spoon over some Tomato Salsa, then some sour cream, sprinkle with grated Cheddar cheese and garnish with coriander.

TOMATO SALSA
Makes about 300 ml/10 fl oz/1¼ cups

1 small onion, chopped
1 garlic clove, crushed
2 fresh green chillies, seeded and finely
    chopped, or 5 ml/1 tsp bottled
    chopped chillies
450 g/1 lb tomatoes, skinned
    and chopped
salt
30 ml/2 tbsp chopped fresh coriander
    (cilantro)

Stir all the ingredients together until well mixed.

Chinese Duck in Pitta

This recipe is based on Chinese crispy duck but uses just the duck breast, which will have a pinkish tinge. If you like it well cooked, leave it in the oven for a further 5 minutes.

Makes 2

1 duck breast, weighing about 175 g/6 oz
3 spring onions (scallions)
7.5 cm/3 in piece cucumber
2 round pitta breads
30 ml/2 tbsp hoi-sin sauce
radish chrysanthemum and spring onion
    (scallion) tassel, to garnish

1 Preheat the oven to 220°C/425°F/gas mark 7. Skin the duck breast, place the skin and breast separately on a rack and cook in the oven for 10 minutes.

2 Remove the skin from the oven and slice. Return to the oven for 5 minutes.

3 Meanwhile cut the spring onions (scallions) and cucumber into fine shreds about 4 cm/1½ in long.

4 Heat the pitta bread in the oven for a few minutes until puffed up, then split in half to make a pocket.

5 Slice the duck breast thinly.

6 Stuff the duck breast into the pitta bread with a little spring onion, cucumber, crispy duck skin and some hoi-sin sauce. Serve garnished with a radish chrysanthemum and spring onion tassel.

COOK'S TIP
Duck legs could be used instead for this dish, but they will take longer to cook: for crisp skin, allow about 1 hour at 200°C/400°F/gas 6. Prick the skin all over, lightly salt it then place on a rack over a roasting pan in the oven. Drain off excess fat when necessary.

Tuna Melt

Melts can also be made with a variety of meats such as salami, pastrami beef or chicken, then covered with cheese and griddled or grilled (broiled).

Makes 2

90 g/3½ oz can tuna fish, drained and
   roughly flaked
30 ml/2 tbsp mayonnaise
15 ml/1 tbsp finely chopped celery
15 ml/1 tbsp finely chopped spring
   onion (scallion)
15 ml/1 tbsp chopped fresh parsley
5 ml/1 tsp lemon juice
25 g/1 oz/2 tbsp softened butter
4 slices wholemeal (wholewheat) bread
50 g/2 oz Gruyère or Emmenthal (Swiss)
   cheese, sliced
celery leaves and radish roses, to garnish

1 Mix together the tuna fish, mayonnaise, celery, spring onion (scallion), parsley and lemon juice.

2 Butter the bread with half the butter and spread 2 of them with tuna filling. Top with cheese slices, then bread.

3 Butter the bread on top. Grill (broil) for 1–2 minutes. Turn, spread with the remaining butter and grill for 1–2 minutes until the cheese begins to melt. Garnish with celery leaves and radish roses.

PASTRAMI MELT

Arrange 2 slices pastrami on a slice of rye bread and spread with mustard. Cover with tomato and onion slices, top with cheese, cover with the buttered bread and griddle or grill (broil) on both sides.

Reuben Sandwich

A popular New York Jewish creation, that combines rye bread or pumpernickel, salt beef, Gruyère (Swiss) cheese and sauerkraut. The sandwich should be crisp and hot outside and cold inside.

Makes 2

25 g/1 oz/2 tbsp softened butter
4 slices rye bread or pumpernickel
50 g/2 oz wafer-thin salt beef
50 g/2 oz Gruyère (Swiss) cheese, sliced
15 ml/1 tbsp tomato ketchup
30 ml/2 tbsp mayonnaise
90 ml/6 tbsp sauerkraut
sliced gherkins (dill pickles) and celery
    leaves, to garnish

1 Butter the bread and top 2 slices with beef then put cheese on the other slices.

2 Mix the tomato ketchup and mayonnaise with the sauerkraut.

3 Pile the sauerkraut mixture on top of the cheese and spread to the edges.

COOK'S TIP
You can substitute corned beef for the salt beef, and add piquancy to the sauerkraut with 2.5ml/½ tsp each horseradish sauce and Worcestershire sauce.

4 Lay the other slices, beef side down, on top of the sauerkraut. Butter the bread on top, then grill (broil) for 1–2 minutes until crisp. Turn over, butter the second side and grill for a further 1–2 minutes until the cheese just begins to melt. Serve garnished with gherkin (dill pickle) slices and celery leaves.

Köfte in Pitta Pockets

Köfte is the Turkish name for meatballs. These are made with minced (ground) lamb spiced with cumin, then served with salad in warmed pitta bread.

Makes 4

1 slice white bread
225 g/8 oz minced (ground) lamb
1 garlic clove, crushed
1 small onion, finely chopped
5 ml/1 tsp ground cumin
15 ml/1 tbsp chopped fresh mint
salt and pepper
15 ml/1 tbsp pine nuts
flour for coating
oil for shallow-frying
4 pitta breads
1 onion, cut into thin rings
2 tomatoes, sliced or cut into wedges

1 Preheat the oven to 220°C/425°F/gas mark 7. Soak the bread in water for 5 minutes, then squeeze dry and add to the next 7 ingredients. Mix until thoroughly blended and malleable. Shape into small balls the size of a walnut, using dampened hands so that the mixture does not stick. Coat in flour.

2 Shallow-fry for about 6 minutes, turning frequently, until golden brown.

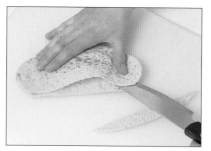

3 Heat the pitta bread in the oven for a few minutes until puffed up, then cut a thin strip off one side of each pitta to make a pocket.

4 Fill with onion rings, tomato wedges and a few Köfte.

TZATZIKI

Mix together 100 g/4 oz/1½ cups Greek (plain) yogurt, 50 g/2 oz/⅓ cup peeled and grated cucumber, 1 crushed garlic clove, 15 ml/1 tbsp chopped fresh mint and seasoning to taste.

LAMB IN PITTA POCKETS

Mix together 50 ml/2 fl oz/¼ cup red wine, 50 ml/2 fl oz/¼ cup olive oil, 2 chopped garlic cloves, 1 bay leaf and ½ teaspoon each of ground cumin and ground coriander. Marinade a 175g/6 oz lamb fillet in this mixture for at least 30 minutes. Grill (broil) for 10 minutes, turning once, then slice thinly and stuff into a warmed pitta pocket with salad and Tzatziki.

Chilli Beef Tacos

A taco is a soft wheat or corn tortilla wrapped around a spicy warm filling of beef and hot peppers. It could be described as a Mexican sandwich.

Makes 4

15 ml/1 tbsp oil
1 small onion, chopped
2 garlic cloves, chopped
175 g/6 oz/¾ cup minced (ground) beef
7 ml/½ tbsp flour
200 g/7 oz can tomatoes
7 ml/½ tbsp Jalapeño peppers,
    finely chopped
salt
4 wheat or corn tortillas
45 ml/3 tbsp sour cream
½ avocado, peeled, stoned (pitted)
    and sliced
1 tomato, sliced
Tomato Salsa (*see* page 30), to serve
    (optional)

1 Heat the oil in a frying-pan (skillet), add the onion and fry until softened. Add the garlic and beef and cook, stirring constantly so that the meat is broken up as it seals.

2 Stir in the flour, then add the canned tomatoes, peppers and salt to taste.

3 Heat the tortillas one at a time in a medium-hot lightly oiled pan.

4 Spread a spoonful of the meat mixture over each tortilla.

5 Top each tortilla with some sour cream and avocado and tomato slices. Roll up and serve immediately with Tomato Salsa if liked.

COOK'S TIP
Instead of beef, try minced chicken in these tacos. Or fried prawns (shrimp) would also work well.

Toasted Pizza-topped Scones

Use whatever cheese you have to hand – Cheddar, mozzarella or goat's cheese will all work well. Add a few olives too, if you like. If you prefer, substitute bought scones for home-made ones.

Makes 12

6 Cheese and Herb Scones
90 ml/6 tbsp red pesto
2 tomatoes, sliced
5 ml/1 tsp dried oregano
salt and pepper
225 g/8 oz/2 cups grated Cheddar cheese

1 Cut the scones in half, toast on the cut side and spread with red pesto.

2 Put a slice of tomato on each one and sprinkle with the oregano and seasoning to taste.

3 Pile grated cheese on top of each one and place under a moderate grill (broiler) until brown and bubbling.

COOK'S TIP
Add a selection of toppings to the scone bases: try mushrooms, anchovies, Italian sausage, pepperoni or peppers and onions.

CHEESE AND HERB SCONES
These scones are so quick to make, and when cut in half make tasty bases for grilled (broiled) toppings.

Makes 6

225 g/8 oz/2 cups self-raising
   (self-rising) flour
5 ml/1 tsp mustard powder
cayenne pepper
2.5 ml/½ tsp salt
50 g/2 oz/4 tbsp butter
5 ml/1 tsp dried oregano
75 g/3 oz/¾ cup grated Cheddar cheese
100 ml/4 fl oz/½ cup milk, plus extra

Preheat the oven to 220°C/425°F/gas mark 7. Sift the flour, mustard, cayenne and salt into a bowl. Rub in the butter until the mixture resembles breadcrumbs. Mix in the oregano and cheese, then add the milk and mix to a soft dough. Turn on to a floured surface, knead and roll out to a thickness of 1 cm/½ in. Cut into 7.5 cm/3 in rounds with a cutter, place on a floured baking sheet and brush with milk. Bake for 12–15 minutes until golden. Cool.

Ciabatta Rolls with Goat's Cheese

The Tomato Relish adds a piquant bite that nicely complements the goat's cheese. If you can't find ciabatta rolls, use a ciabatta loaf instead.

Makes 4

2 ciabatta rolls
60 ml/4 tbsp Tomato Relish
30 ml/2 tbsp chopped fresh basil
175 g/6 oz goat's cheese, thinly sliced
6 black olives, halved and stoned (pitted)
1 sprig fresh basil, to garnish

1 Cut the rolls in half and toast on one side only.

2 Spread a little relish over each half and sprinkle with the chopped basil.

3 Arrange the goat's cheese slices on this and scatter a few olives over the top. Place under a hot grill (broiler) until the goat's cheese begins to melt, then serve garnished with a sprig of basil.

TOMATO RELISH
Makes 450 ml/15 fl oz/scant 2 cups

45 ml/3 tbsp olive oil
1 onion, chopped
1 red (bell) pepper, seeded and chopped
2 garlic cloves
¼ tsp chilli powder
400 g/14 oz can chopped tomatoes
15 ml/1 tbsp clear honey
10 ml/2 tsp black olive paste
30 ml/2 tbsp red wine vinegar
salt and pepper

Heat the oil and fry the onion and red (bell) pepper until softened. Add the garlic and the remaining ingredients, and season to taste. Simmer for 15 minutes until the mixture has thickened.

Ciabatta with Mozzarella and Onion

This tasty open sandwich is so simple to make, and you can vary the ingredients depending on what is in your store cupboard or refrigerator.

Makes 4

1 ciabatta loaf
60 ml/4 tbsp red pesto
2 small onions
oil, for brushing
225 g/8 oz mozzarella cheese
8 black olives

1 Cut the bread in half horizontally and toast lightly. Spread with the red pesto.

COOK'S TIP
Ciabatta is also delicious made with spinach, sun-dried tomatoes or olives.

2 Peel the onions and cut horizontally into thick slices. Brush with oil and grill (broil) for 3 minutes until lightly browned.

3 Slice the cheese and arrange on the bread. Add onion slices and scatter with olives. Cut in half diagonally. Place under a hot grill for 2–3 minutes until the cheese melts and the onion chars.

Welsh Rarebit

This recipe is traditionally made with brown ale (beer) or red wine, which gives it a delicious flavour. If you put a poached or fried egg on top, the dish becomes a Buck Rarebit.

2 Heat gently, stirring constantly, until the cheese is just beginning to melt.

3 Meanwhile toast the bread. Spread the cheese mixture over the toast.

4 Grill (broil) lightly until tinged brown here and there.

Makes 4

100 g/4 oz/1 cup grated mature (sharp)
   Cheddar cheese
30 ml/2 tbsp brown ale (beer)
5 ml/1 tsp English mustard
cayenne pepper
4 slices bread

COOK'S TIP
Welsh Rarebit is equally good with other cheeses such as Stilton or Red Leicester.

1 Put the cheese in a saucepan with the brown ale (beer), mustard and cayenne pepper and mix together thoroughly.

Crostini with Tomato and Anchovy

Crostini are little rounds of bread cut from a French stick and toasted or fried, then covered with a tasty topping such as melted cheese, olive paste, anchovy, tomato or chicken liver.

Makes 8

1 small French stick (large enough to give
   8 slices)
30 ml/2 tbsp olive oil
2 garlic cloves, chopped
4 tomatoes, skinned and chopped
15 ml/1 tbsp chopped fresh basil
15 ml/1 tbsp tomato purée (paste)
salt and pepper
8 canned anchovy fillets
12 black olives, halved and stoned (pitted)
1 sprig fresh basil, to garnish

1 Cut the loaf diagonally into 8 slices about 1 cm/½ in thick and toast until golden on both sides.

2 Heat the oil and fry the garlic and tomatoes for 4 minutes. Stir in the basil, tomato paste and seasoning.

COOK'S TIP
To vary the toppings, spread the toasted bread with pesto then top with either mozzarella balls or sliced mozzarella. Sprinkle with a little oil and chopped basil.

3 Spoon a little tomato mixture on to each slice of bread. Place an anchovy fillet on each one and sprinkle with olives. Serve garnished with a sprig of basil.

CROSTINI WITH ONION AND OLIVE
Fry 350 g/12 oz/2 cups sliced onions in 30 ml/2 tbsp olive oil till golden brown. Stir in 8 roughly chopped anchovy fillets, 12 halved, stoned (pitted) black olives, some seasoning and 5 ml/1 tsp dried thyme. Spread the toasted bread with 15 ml/1 tbsp black olive paste and spread a spoonful of the onion mixture over each one.

Focaccia with Hot Artichokes and Olives

Focaccia makes an excellent base for different grilled (broiled) toppings. Artichoke hearts bottled in oil with pepper, oregano and pepperoni are a tasty combination.

Makes 3

60 ml/4 tbsp olive paste
3 Olive Focaccia
1 small red (bell) pepper, halved and
    seeded
275 g/10 oz bottled or canned artichoke
    hearts, drained
75 g/3 oz pepperoni, sliced
5 ml/1 tsp dried oregano

1 Preheat the oven to 220°C/425°F/gas mark 7. Spread the olive paste over the focaccia. Grill (broil) the red pepper till blackened, put in a plastic bag, seal and allow to cool for 10 minutes. Skin the pepper and cut into strips.

2 Quarter the artichoke hearts and arrange over the paste with the pepperoni.

3 Sprinkle over the red pepper strips and the oregano. Place in the oven for 5–10 minutes until heated through.

OLIVE FOCACCIA

Focaccia is an Italian flat bread made with olive oil and sometimes with olives, too. The amount of water needed varies with the type of flour used, so you may need a less or more – than the given quantity.

Makes 6 focaccia

450 g/1 lb/4 cups strong white
    (bread) flour
5 ml/1 tsp salt
5 ml/1 tsp dried yeast
pinch of sugar
300 ml/10 fl oz/1¼ cups warm water
60 ml/4 tbsp olive oil
100 g/4 oz/1 cup black olives, stoned
    (pitted) and roughly chopped
2.5 ml/½ tsp dried oregano

1 Mix the flour and salt in a mixing bowl. Put the yeast in a small bowl and mix with half the water and a pinch of sugar. Leave for about 10 minutes until dissolved. Add the yeast mixture to the flour with the oil, olives and remaining water and mix to a soft dough, adding a little more water if necessary.

2 Turn the dough out on to a floured surface and knead for 5 minutes until it is smooth and elastic. Place in a mixing bowl, cover with a damp tea (dish) towel and leave in a warm place to rise for about 2 hours or until doubled in size.

3 Preheat the oven to 220°C/425°F/ gas mark 7. Turn the dough out on to a floured surface and knead for a few minutes. Divide into 6, then roll out each to a thickness of 1 cm/½ in in a round or oblong shape. Place on an oiled baking sheet. Make indentations over the surface and sprinkle with the oregano. Bake in the oven for 12–15 minutes.

Pan Bagnat

This literally means 'bathed bread' and is basically a Salade Niçoise stuffed into a baguette or roll. The olive oil dressing soaks into the bread when it is left with a weight on top of it.

Makes 4

1 large baguette
150 ml/5 fl oz/²⁄₃ cup French Dressing
1 small onion, thinly sliced
3 tomatoes, sliced
1 small green or red (bell) pepper, seeded
    and sliced
50 g/2 oz can anchovy fillets, drained
90 g/3½ oz can tuna fish, drained
50 g/2 oz black olives, halved and
    stoned (pitted)

1 Split the baguette horizontally along one side without cutting all the way through the crust.

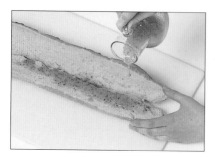

2 Open the bread out so that it lies flat and sprinkle the French Dressing evenly over the top.

COOK'S TIP
For a variation, add to the pan bagnat 2 shelled and sliced hard-boiled eggs, 6 radishes, sliced and 15ml/1 tbsp fresh basil, torn into pieces.

3 Arrange the onion, tomatoes, green or red pepper, anchovies, tuna and olives on one side of the bread. Close the 2 halves, pressing firmly together.

4 Wrap in clear film (plastic wrap), lay a board on top, put a weight on it and leave for about I hour: as well as allowing the dressing to soak into the bread, this makes it easier to eat.

5 Using a serrated bread knife, cut the loaf diagonally into 4 equal portions.

FRENCH DRESSING
Olive oil is a must for this dressing; it imparts a rich, fruity flavour, especially if you use that lovely green, virgin olive oil. Make a large quantity at a time and store it in a wine bottle, ready for instant use.

Makes about 450 ml/¾ pint/scant 2 cups

350 ml/12 fl oz/1½ cups extra-virgin
    olive oil
90 ml/6 tbsp red wine vinegar
15 ml/1 tbsp Moutarde de Meaux
1 garlic clove, crushed
5 ml/1 tsp clear honey
salt and pepper

Pour the olive oil into a measuring jug and make up to 450 ml/¾ pint/scant 2 cups with the vinegar. Add the remaining ingredients, then, using a funnel pour into a wine bottle. Put in the cork firmly, give the mixture a thorough shake and store.

Ciabatta Sandwich

If you can find a ciabatta with sun-dried tomatoes, it improves the flavour of the sandwich. Parma ham should be very thinly sliced and then cut into strips to make it easier to eat.

Makes 3

60 ml/4 tbsp mayonnaise
30 ml/2 tbsp pesto
1 ciabatta loaf
100 g/4 oz provolone or mozzarella
    cheese, sliced
75 g/3 oz Parma ham, cut into strips
4 plum tomatoes, sliced
sprigs fresh basil, torn into pieces

1 Thoroughly mix together the mayonnaise and pesto sauce.

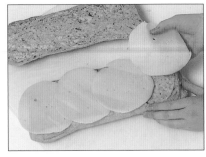

2 Cut the ciabatta in half horizontally and spread the cut side of both halves with the pesto mayonnaise. Lay the cheese over one half of the ciabatta.

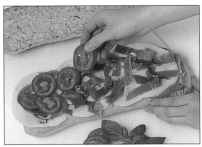

3 Cut the Parma ham into strips and arrange over the top. Cover with the sliced tomatoes and torn basil leaves. Sandwich together with the other half and cut into 3 pieces.

COOK'S TIP
If you like your sandwiches to have more of a kick, deseed and finely chop 1 red chilli and stir it into the filling.

Frankfurter and Potato Salad Sandwich

An unlikely mixture to put into a sandwich, but one that works extremely well. If the potato salad is a bit too chunky, chop it a little first. This is best eaten with a knife and fork.

Makes 2

100 g/4 oz/²/₃ cup potato salad
2 spring onions (scallions), chopped
25 g/1 oz/2 tbsp softened butter
4 slices wholemeal (wholewheat) bread
4 frankfurters
2 tomatoes, sliced

1 Mix the potato salad with the spring onions (scallions).

2 Butter all 4 slices of bread and divide the potato salad equally between 2 of them, spreading it to the edges.

3 Slice the frankfurters diagonally and arrange over the potato salad with the tomato slices.

4 Sandwich with the remaining bread, press together lightly and cut in half.

FRANKFURTER AND EGG FILLING
Shell and roughly chop 1 hard-boiled egg and mix with 15 ml/1 tbsp mayonnaise and 15 ml/1 tbsp chopped fresh chives. Use in place of the potato salad.

Omelette Roll

This is an unusual way to serve an omelette but it is good either warm or cold. It's equally good made with wholemeal (wholewheat) bread, in which case don't roll the omelette.

Makes 1

1 Cheese and Tomato Stick (*see* page 12)
10 ml/2 tsp crushed sun-dried tomatoes
2 eggs
salt and pepper
few sprigs watercress
30 ml/2 tbsp chopped fresh chives
15 ml/1 tbsp chopped sun-dried
    tomatoes
15 g/½ oz/1 tbsp butter

1 Slice the roll horizontally, scoop out some of the crumb to make a hollow, and spread the crushed sun-dried tomato over the bread.

2 Break the eggs into a small bowl, add seasoning, 15 ml/1 tbsp water, the watercress, chives, and chopped sun-dried tomato and whisk with a fork.

3 Heat the butter in a small omelette pan until it sizzles.

4 Tip in the egg, then, as it begins to set, draw the sides toward the middle, so that more egg touches the hot pan. Repeat this a couple more times.

5 When the egg is just set, lift the edge of the omelette nearest the handle, tilting the pan away from you.

6 Flip the omelette over and gently slip it into the roll.

COOK'S TIP
An omelette roll makes a substantial breakfast dish, perfect food on the move. For an even heartier dish, add a rasher (strip) of grilled bacon.

Salami Hero

This is a hearty sandwich, filled with as much as you can cram into a roll. An American speciality that varies regionally, it can contain tuna, egg, cheese, coleslaw, salads, meats or salamis.

2 Arrange lettuce or radicchio leaves on the base, then add a spoonful of coleslaw.

3 Fold the salami slices in half and arrange over the top. Cover with a little more lettuce, tomato slices and a little mayonnaise.

Makes 2

2 long crusty rolls
25 g/1 oz/2 tbsp softened butter
few leaves lollo rosso lettuce or radicchio
75 g/3 oz coleslaw
75 g/3 oz Italian salami, sliced
1 tomato, sliced
30 ml/2 tbsp mayonnaise

COOK'S TIP
Serve the salami hero with a napkin to mop up the juices from the coleslaw and mayonnaise.

1 Cut the rolls horizontally three-quarters of the way through, open out enough to take the filling and butter both cut sides.

Classic BLT

This delicious American sandwich is made with crispy fried bacon, lettuce and tomato. Choose the bread you prefer and toast it if you like.

Makes 2

4 slices granary bread
15 g/½ oz/1 tbsp softened butter
few crisp lettuce leaves, cos or iceberg
1 large tomato, sliced
8 rashers (slices) streaky bacon
30 ml/2 tbsp mayonnaise

1 Spread 2 of the slices of bread with butter. Lay the lettuce over the bread and cover with sliced tomato.

COOK'S TIP
As a variation from the classic BLT, add 10ml/2 tsp Dijon mustard to the mayonnaise, and slice an avocado for the filling.

2 Grill (broil) the bacon until it begins to crisp, then arrange it over the lettuce and sliced tomato.

3 Spread the 2 remaining slices of bread with mayonnaise. Lay over the bacon, press the sandwich together gently and cut in half.

Club Sandwich

Club sandwiches, or triple-deckers, are made with 3 layers of bread and should be generously filled. The filling can be chicken, ham, cheese or beef, with a relish, salad and mayonnaise.

Makes 1

25 g/1 oz/2 tbsp softened butter
2 slices brown bread
1 slice white bread
2 slices rare roast beef
5 ml/1 tsp Horseradish Relish
few leaves curly endive
1 tomato, sliced
½ avocado, peeled and sliced
30 ml/2 tbsp mayonnaise
carrot curls and stuffed olives, to garnish

1 Butter the brown bread on one side only and the white bread on both sides.

2 Cover one of the brown slices with 2 slices beef, some Horseradish Relish and then some curly endive.

COOK'S TIP
Try toasting the bread for this sandwich, as it was in the original recipe. As it is a double decker, it is easier to eat this sandwich using a knife and fork.

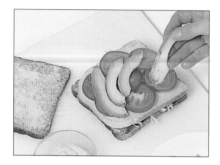

3 Cover this layer with the white bread and then arrange tomato and avocado slices on top.

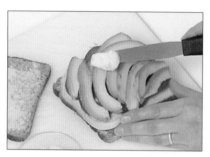

4 Spread mayonnaise over the top, and sandwich with the remaining brown slice of bread.

5 Press together lightly and cut into quarters.

6 Put carrot curls and stuffed olives on cocktail sticks (toothpicks) and stick into each sandwich to garnish.

HORSERADISH RELISH
Makes about 75 ml/3 fl oz/⅓ cup

45 ml/3 tbsp fromage frais or ricotta cheese
20 ml/4 tsp grainy mustard
20 ml/4 tsp horseradish sauce

Mix all ingredients together in a bowl.

Prawn, Tomato and Mayonnaise Sandwich

Use frozen cold-water prawns (shrimp) for the best taste, and make quite sure that they are thoroughly defrosted, well drained and patted dry before you assemble the sandwich.

Makes 2

25 g/1 oz/2 tbsp softened butter
5 ml/1 tsp sun-dried tomato paste
4 slices wholemeal (wholewheat) bread
1 bunch watercress, trimmed
45 ml/3 tbsp Tomato Mayonnaise
100 g/4 oz/⅔ cup frozen cooked peeled
    prawns (shrimp), defrosted

1 Mix the butter and tomato paste together until well blended.

2 Spread on the bread and then arrange sprigs of watercress on 2 of the slices.

3 Spread Tomato Mayonnaise to the edges, then sprinkle the prawns (shrimp) over the top. Sandwich with the remaining bread slices and cut in quarters.

TOMATO MAYONNAISE
Makes 175 ml/6 fl oz/¾ cup

Skin, seed and chop 1 tomato and place in a blender with 1 small crushed garlic clove, 1 tsp soft brown sugar and 10 ml/2 tsp tomato purée (paste). Blend and stir into 100 ml/4 fl oz/½ cup mayonnaise.

Chicken and Curry Mayonnaise Sandwich

A very useful and appetizing way of using leftover pieces of chicken. This filling would work just as well for other cold meats, such as turkey or ham.

Makes 2

4 slices granary bread
25 g/1 oz/2 tbsp softened butter
100 g/4 oz/1 cup cooked chicken, sliced
45 ml/3 tbsp Curry Mayonnaise
1 bunch watercress, trimmed

1 Spread the bread with butter and arrange the chicken over 2 of the slices.

CURRY MAYONNAISE
Makes about 150 ml/5 fl oz/²/₃ cup

100 ml/4 fl oz/¹/₂ cup mayonnaise
10 ml/2 tsp concentrated curry sauce
2.5 ml/¹/₂ tsp lemon juice
10 ml/2 tsp sieved (strained) apricot jam

Mix all the ingredients together thoroughly.

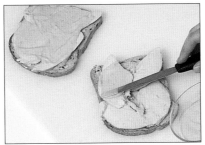

2 Spread Curry Mayonnaise over the chicken slices.

3 Arrange sprigs of watercress on top, cover with the remaining bread, press lightly together and cut in half.

Crab and Avocado Sandwich

The combination of succulent crab meat and avocado works very successfully in this delicious sandwich. Fresh crab meat is best but frozen or canned can also be used.

Makes 4

175 g/6 oz fresh crab meat or canned in
    brine, drained
2 spring onions (scallions), chopped
salt and pepper
100 ml/4 fl oz/½ cup mayonnaise
1 large avocado, peeled and halved
15 ml/1 tbsp lemon juice
50 g/2 oz/4 tbsp softened butter
8 slices granary bread
endive leaves, to garnish

1 Mix the crab meat with the spring onions (scallions), seasoning and 30 ml/ 2 tbsp of the mayonnaise.

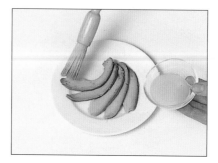

2 Cut the avocado into slices and brush with lemon juice.

3 Butter the bread and divide the crab meat between 4 of the slices, spreading it to the edges.

4 Arrange the slices of avocado over the crab.

5 Spread the remaining mayonnaise over the top. Cover with the remaining bread slices and press together firmly. Cut off the crusts and cut the sandwiches diagonally into quarters. Garnish with endive leaves.

COOK'S TIP
Add a Caribbean twist to this sandwich by adding 15ml/2 tbsp chopped fresh coriander (cilantro), the juice of half a lime and 1 green chilli, deseeded and finely chopped.

Oriental Chicken Sandwich

This filling is also good served in warmed pitta bread, in which case cut the chicken into small cubes before marinating, grill (broil) on skewers and serve warm.

Makes 2

15 ml/1 tbsp soy sauce
5 ml/1 tsp clear honey
5 ml/1 tsp sesame oil
1 garlic clove, crushed
175 g/6 oz skinless boneless
    chicken breast
4 slices white bread
60 ml/4 tbsp Peanut Sauce (*see* page 17)
25 g/1 oz/¼ cup beansprouts
25 g/1 oz/¼ cup red (bell) pepper, seeded
    and finely sliced
2 sprigs parsley, to garnish

1 Mix together the soy sauce, honey, sesame oil and garlic. Brush over the chicken breast.

2 Grill (broil) the chicken for 3–4 minutes on each side until cooked through, then slice thinly.

3 Spread 2 slices of the bread with some of the Peanut Sauce.

COOK'S TIP

For a vegetarian version of this sandwich, omit the chicken and substitute 175g/6oz shredded cabbage, 2 grated carrots and 15ml/1 tbsp each chopped fresh coriander (cilantro) and mint leaves. Instead of white bread, slice up a baguette and add the filling.

4 Arrange the chicken slices over the sauce-covered bread.

5 Spread a little more peanut sauce over the chicken.

6 Sprinkle over the beansprouts and red (bell) pepper and sandwich together with the remaining slices of bread. Garnish with parsley.

Tuna and Sweetcorn Bap

Tuna and corn make a delicious combination. It's a rather soft filling, so it is better served in a roll, which is firmer to hold, than between slices of bread.

2 Cut the baps in half and divide the filling between each bottom half.

3 Place a lettuce leaf on top, cover with the remaining Tartare Sauce and replace the top of each bap.

Makes 2

90 g/3½ oz canned tuna fish, drained and flaked
90 ml/6 tbsp cooked corn kernels
60 ml/4 tbsp chopped cucumber
2 spring onions (scallions), chopped
90 ml/6 tbsp Tartare Sauce
2 granary baps (rolls)
2 green or lollo rosso lettuce leaves

1 Mix together the tuna fish, corn, cucumber, spring onions and 30 ml/2 tbsp of the Tartare Sauce.

TARTARE SAUCE
Mix together 90 ml/6 tbsp mayonnaise with 10 ml/2 tsp each of chopped gherkins (dill pickle), chopped capers and chopped parsley.

Bagels and Lox

Bagels should be served warm, with a traditional filling of smoked salmon and cream cheese, but other fillings also work well, particularly smoked mackerel.

Makes 2

2 bagels
100 g/4 oz/½ cup cream cheese
5 ml/1 tsp lemon juice
15 ml/1 tbsp chopped fresh chives
salt and pepper
a little milk (optional)
100 g/4 oz smoked salmon
dill sprigs and lemon slices, to garnish

2 Cut the bagels in half horizontally and spread the bases with the cream cheese.

3 Arrange the smoked salmon over the cream cheese and replace the tops of the bagels. Garnish with lemon and dill.

1 Preheat the oven to 180°C/350°F/gas mark 4. Wrap the bagels in foil and warm through in the oven for 10 minutes. Mix the cream cheese with the lemon juice, chives, seasoning and a little milk to thin if necessary.

Farmer's Brunch

A new twist to a traditional, wholesome sandwich. Use fresh crusty white bread and top the cheese with a home-made Peach Relish, which goes particularly well with Red Leicester cheese.

Makes 2

4 slices crusty white bread
25 g/1 oz/2 tbsp softened butter
100 g/4 oz Red Leicester or Wensleydale
    cheese (Monterey Jack or
    Tilamook), sliced
45 ml/3 tbsp Peach Relish
spring onions (scallions), or pickled
    onions, and tomato wedges, to serve

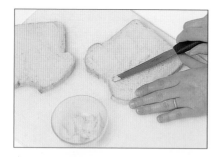

1 Butter the bread.

2 Cover 2 slices with cheese slices.

3 Spread Peach Relish over the remaining 2 slices and place them over the cheese.

5 Cut in half and serve with spring onions or pickled onions, and tomato wedges.

PEACH RELISH
A very quick relish that can be eaten immediately. It will keep up to 1 month in the refrigerator.

Makes about 700 ml/25 fl oz/3 cups relish

60 ml/4 tbsp wine vinegar
60 ml/4 tbsp light soft brown sugar
5 ml/1 tsp finely chopped chilli
5 ml/1 tsp finely chopped ginger
5 peaches, stoned (pitted) and chopped
1 yellow (bell) pepper, seeded
    and chopped
1 small onion, chopped

1 Put the vinegar and sugar in a saucepan with the chilli and ginger and heat gently until the sugar has dissolved.

2 Add the remaining ingredients and bring to the boil, stirring constantly.

3 Cover and cook gently for 15 minutes. Remove the lid and cook for a further 10–15 minutes until tender and the liquid is slightly reduced. Pour into warm, clean jars and cover.

Baguette with Pâté

This lovely picnic sandwich is filled with pork or duck rillettes, a rich mixture of shredded meat, or try a pâté of your choice. It is also delicious filled with Brie or Camembert cheese.

Makes 2

2 demi-baguettes
25 g/1 oz/2 tbsp softened butter
2 tomatoes, sliced
5 cm/2 in piece cucumber, sliced
few lettuce leaves
100 g/4 oz Country Pâté or pork rillettes

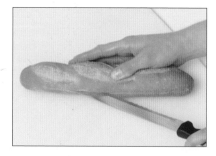

1 Cut the demi-baguettes three-quarters of the way through horizontally and spread the cut sides with butter.

2 Fill with a layer of tomato and cucumber slices. Lay the lettuce leaves over the top.

3 Spoon half the rillettes or pâté into each baguette and press the baguette halves together firmly.

BRIE AND TOMATO BAGUETTE
Put a little lettuce and a few tomato slices in the baguette, then top with 50 g/2 oz ripe Brie slices and a few stoned (pitted) black olives.

COUNTRY PÂTÉ
Makes about 900 g/2 lb

225 g/8 oz streaky bacon rashers (slices), rind removed
350 g/12 oz/3 cups minced (ground) pork
225 g/8 oz pig's liver, minced (ground)
100 g/4 oz pork sausagemeat
1 onion, finely chopped
2 garlic cloves, crushed
5 ml/1 tsp chopped fresh thyme
15 ml/1 tbsp chopped fresh parsley
salt and pepper

1 Preheat the oven to 170°C/325°F/gas mark 3. Stretch the bacon with a palette knife (spatula) and use three-quarters of it to line a 900 ml/1½ pint/3¾ cup terrine. Set the remaining bacon aside.

2 Put the rest of the ingredients in a bowl and mix together thoroughly, or combine them in a food processor. Turn into the terrine and smooth the top. Cover with the remaining bacon.

3 Cover with a lid, or foil, and place in a roasting tin (roasting pan) half-filled with water and cook in the oven for 1¼ –1½ hours.

4 Remove the lid or foil, cover with greaseproof paper (baking parchment), place a 1 kg/2¼ lb weight on top and leave until cold.

Herring and Apple on Rye

For these open sandwiches, you can use rollmops, herrings in wine sauce or any other type of pickled herrings of your choice. Gherkins, apples and tomatoes are arranged on top.

Makes 4

25 g/1 oz/2 tbsp softened butter
4 slices rye bread
few lettuce leaves
4 pickled herring fillets
1 red apple, cored and sliced
5 ml/1 tsp lemon juice
60 ml/4 tbsp Fennel and Sour Cream
    Dressing (see page 17)
fennel sprigs, to garnish

1 Spread the butter on the bread and cover with a few lettuce leaves.

2 Cut the herring fillets in half and arrange on top.

3 Brush the apple slices with lemon juice and arrange round the herring.

4 Spoon over some Fennel and Sour Cream Dressing and garnish with fennel.

COOK'S TIP
Herring is quite rich, so needs strong-tasting ingredients to mix into sandwich toppings. Horseradish and capers would both be good additions.

HERRING, POTATO AND GHERKIN (DILL PICKLE)
Put 15 ml/1 tbsp potato salad on a lettuce leaf, arrange a herring fillet on top and garnish with sliced gherkin (dill pickle) and cherry tomatoes. Top with a fennel sprig.

BEETROOT, HERRING AND ONION
Put some sliced cooked beetroot over the lettuce, arrange a herring fillet on top and garnish with thinly sliced onion rings, Fennel and Sour Cream Dressing and a fennel sprig.

Ham and Asparagus Slice

Be creative in your arrangement of the ingredients here. You could make ham cornets, or wrap the asparagus in the ham, or use different meats such as salami, mortadella or Black Forest ham.

Makes 4

12 asparagus spears
100 g/4 oz/½ cup cream cheese
4 slices rye bread
4 slices ham
few leaves curly endive
30 ml/2 tbsp mayonnaise
4 radish roses, to garnish

1 Cook the asparagus until tender, drain, pat dry with kitchen paper and cool.

2 Spread cream cheese over the rye bread and arrange the ham in folds over the top.

3 Lay 3 asparagus spears on each sandwich.

4 Arrange curly endive on top of the spears and spoon over some mayonnaise.

COOK'S TIP
Asparagus is at its best in season. Select firm, straight spears that have closed tips. Bend to snap off the woody ends, then rinse and steam in an upright position for around 5–7 minutes until the asparagus is tender.

5 Garnish with radish roses and serve extra mayonnaise separately in a small bowl if liked.

SALAMI AND COTTAGE CHEESE SLICE
Omit the asparagus. Arrange 3 salami slices over the rye bread with a spoonful of cottage cheese and chopped fresh chives. Garnish with watercress, chives and chive flowers.

Scrambled Egg and Tomato Fingers

Pumpernickel makes a good firm base for these finger sandwiches and its robust taste combines especially well with that of scrambled egg.

Makes 6

25 g/1 oz/2 tbsp softened butter
2 slices pumpernickel bread
2 eggs
15 ml/1 tbsp milk
salt and pepper
15 ml/1 tbsp single (light) cream
30 ml/2 tbsp chopped fresh chives
mustard and cress
3 canned anchovy fillets, halved
2 sun-dried tomatoes, cut into strips
tomato rose and spring onion (scallion)
    tassel, to garnish

1 Butter the pumpernickel and cut into 6 fingers.

2 Whisk the eggs lightly with the milk and add seasoning to taste. Cook the eggs in a little melted butter over a gentle heat, stirring constantly until lightly scrambled.

3 Stir in the cream and chives, and leave to cool.

4 Arrange a little mustard and cress at the ends of the pumpernickel fingers and spoon over the egg. Place the anchovies and sun-dried tomato strips on top of the egg. Garnish with a tomato rose and spring onion (scallion) tassel.

Smoked Salmon and Gravlax Sauce

Gravlax is Scandinavian marinated salmon, which is traditionally served with a sauce made from mustard, dill and sour cream. The sauce is equally good with smoked salmon, as in this recipe.

Makes 8

25 g/1 oz/2 tbsp softened butter
5 ml/1 tsp grated lemon zest
4 slices rye or pumpernickel bread
100 g/4 oz smoked salmon
few leaves curly endive
lemon slices
cucumber slices
60 ml/4 tbsp Gravlax Sauce (*see* page 15)
dill sprigs, to garnish

1 Mix the butter and lemon zest together, spread over the bread and cut in half diagonally.

2 Arrange the smoked salmon over the top to cover.

3 Add a little curly endive and a lemon and cucumber slice. Spoon over some Gravlax Sauce, then garnish with dill.

Tapenade and Quails' Eggs

Tapenade, a purée made from capers, olives and anchovies, is an excellent partner to eggs. Of course you can use hens' eggs, but quails' eggs look very pretty on open sandwiches.

Makes 8

8 quails' eggs
1 small baguette
45 ml/3 tbsp Tapenade
few leaves curly endive
3 small tomatoes, sliced
4 canned anchovy fillets, halved
    lengthways
black olives
parsley sprigs, to garnish

1 Boil the quails' eggs for 5 minutes, then plunge straight into cold water to cool. Crack the shells and remove them very carefully.

TAPENADE
Makes 300 m1/10 fl oz/1¼ cups
Put a 90 g/3½ oz can drained tuna fish in a food processor with 25 g/1 oz capers, 10 canned anchovy fillets and 75 g/ 3 oz/¾ cup stoned (pitted) black olives and blend until smooth, scraping down the sides as necessary. Gradually add 60 ml/4 tbsp olive oil through the feeder tube and mix well.

2 Cut the baguette into diagonal slices and spread with some Tapenade.

3 Arrange curly endive and tomato slices on top.

4 Halve the quails' eggs and place over the tomato.

5 Finish with a little more Tapenade, the anchovies and olives. Garnish with small parsley sprigs.

COOK'S TIP
Alternative ingredients to add to tapenade include garlic, lemon juice, sun-dried tomatoes, roasted artichokes and aubergines (eggplants), mustard, basil and parsley. To add richness, brandy is sometimes used.

Roquefort and Pear

In this super fast sandwich, Roquefort makes a delicious partner for pear, but other blue cheeses such as Stilton or Cambozola are equally good.

Makes 4

4 slices brioche loaf
125 g/4 oz/½ cup curd (smooth cottage) cheese
few sprigs rocket (arugula)
125 g/4 oz Roquefort cheese, sliced
1 ripe pear, quartered, cored and sliced
juice of ½ lemon
4 pecan nuts, to garnish
viola flowers, to garnish (optional)

1 Toast the brioche and spread with the curd (smooth cottage) cheese.

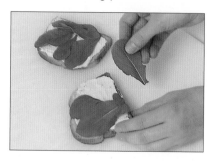

2 Arrange rocket (arugula) leaves on top of the cheese.

3 Place the sliced Roquefort on top.

4 Brush the pear slices with lemon juice to prevent discoloration.

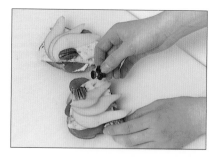

5 Arrange the pear slices, overlapping, in a fan shape on the cheese.

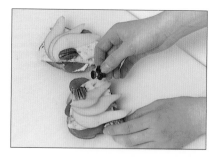

6 Garnish with pecan nuts (whole or chopped) and a viola flower if you wish.

COOK'S TIP
Toasted brioche makes a good base for an open sandwich, but must be eaten straight away, because it quickly becomes soft once the brioche is filled.

Sandwich Train

This is a simple way to make sandwiches more appealing to small children, who sometimes can be fussy about eating. Serving this at a party might inspire kids to take an interest in their food.

Makes 2 trains

2 sandwich rounds made with cream
   cheese or pâté
cucumber skin
radishes
a little sandwich filling
1 celery stick
1 carrot
1 cooked beetroot
cream cheese, lettuce and pretzel stick, to

1 Remove the crusts from the sandwiches and cut each one into 4 squares.

2 Cut the squares in half again to make 8 small sandwiches.

3 Make an engine using 3 of the sandwiches. Arrange the remaining sandwiches behind the engine, placing cucumber strips to resemble tracks.

4 Slice the radishes and stick on to the sides of the train with a little sandwich filling to resemble wheels.

COOK'S TIP
If you are short of time, don't dice the vegetables, leave them in sticks and use them as cargo for the trucks (freight cars).

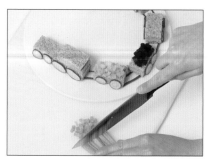

5 Dice the celery, carrot and beetroot and pile on to the trucks (freight cars) to resemble cargo.

6 Cut a carrot funnel, top with cream cheese smoke if liked and place on the engine with half a radish, and a piece of cucumber. If you want to make a tree, tie some lettuce onto a pretzel stick and stick it in position with a blob of cream cheese.

Log Cabin

This takes a little time but is a great favourite with children. If they are old enough, they will probably enjoy helping to make this party sandwich.

Makes 1

4 sandwich rounds made with chosen
    filling, crusts removed
pretzel sticks or wheat sticks with
    yeast extract
50 g/2 oz/¼ cup curd (smooth
    cottage) cheese
1 each tomato, carrot
    and radish
2.5 cm/1 in piece cucumber

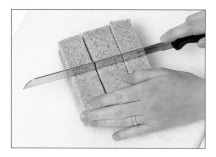

1 Place 2 of the sandwich rounds on a board and cut each into small rectangles.

2 Cut each of the remaining 2 sandwich rounds into 4 triangles.

3 Stack the rectangular sandwiches together to form the cabin and arrange 6 of the triangles on top to form the roof. (Serve the remaining triangles separately.)

4 Arrange pretzel sticks on the roof to look like logs, sticking with a little sandwich filling or curd (smooth cottage) cheese if necessary.

COOK'S TIP
If you can't find pretzel sticks, use chipsticks or bread sticks to form the roof. Just break the sticks to the desired lengths.

5 Break the remaining pretzel sticks into 2.5 cm/1 in lengths and use to make a fence around the cabin, sticking in position with curd cheese.

6 Cut the tomatoes into doors and windows. Cut the carrot into a chimney, attach it using curd cheese and add some curd cheese smoke. Cut flowers from radishes and carrots. Dice the cucumber finely and arrange on the plate to resemble a path.

Sailing Sandwich

A novelty shape may tempt even the most awkward child. The basic sandwich shape is quick and easy to make, though it's a bit more time-consuming to add the trimmings.

Makes 1

1 sandwich round made with
   chosen filling
butter
chopped fresh parsley
few pretzel sticks
paprika
shredded lettuce
tomato ketchup and small pieces of
   lemon rind and cucumber, to
   garnish (optional)

1 Remove the crusts from the sandwich and cut 2 triangular sails from it. Shape the remaining piece of sandwich to resemble a boat.

2 Spread the long edges of the sails with a little butter and dip in chopped parsley.

COOK'S TIP
To make white sails, cut out triangular shapes from a sandwich made from 2 slices of white bread.

3 Turn one sail over and arrange 2 sides together with the pretzel sticks in the centre to represent the mast.

4 Spread the boat shape with butter, dip into paprika and place below the sails. Arrange shredded lettuce underneath to represent the sea. If liked, you can pipe a number on the sail with tomato ketchup Cut out a sun from lemon rind and a flag from cucumber.

Sailing Ships

This novelty sandwich can be prepared with different soft fillings that stand on halved rolls. The processed cheese slices make wonderful sails.

Makes 12

6 bridge rolls
225 g/8 oz chosen filling
chopped fresh parsley
2 tomatoes, quartered and seeded
2 radishes
6 processed cheese slices

1 Cut each roll in half horizontally and trim the base so that it stands evenly. Put 15 ml/1 tbsp of the filling on to each half and spread to the edges, doming it slightly. Make a border with parsley.

2 Cut the tomatoes into thin strips and arrange round the edge of each half-roll.

3 Cut the radishes into strips and 2 triangles. Cut the cheese into sail shapes. Thread each sail on to a cocktail stick (toothpick) and stand in the filling.

PEANUT FILLING
Mix together 45 ml/3 tbsp crunchy peanut butter and 45 ml/3 tbsp tomato chutney.

CHEESE AND PINEAPPLE FILLING
Thoroughly combine 100 g/4 oz/½ cup curd (smooth cottage) cheese and 30 ml/2 tbsp drained and chopped canned pineapple, and add seasoning to taste.

Wigwams

Choose a square-shaped loaf, either brown or white, so that you can cut even-sized triangles; the bread should be thinly sliced, or use a ready-sliced loaf.

Makes 4

4 sandwich rounds made with
    chosen filling
butter
chopped fresh parsley
mustard and cress, or flat-leaf parsley
shredded lettuce
1 red (bell) pepper (optional)
pretzel sticks (optional)

1 Cut each sandwich into triangles.

2 Cut a slanting slice from the base of each triangle so that the sandwich will stand at an angle.

3 Butter one or two of the long sides of the triangles and dip in chopped parsley.

4 Place 4 triangles together to form a wigwam shape.

ANIMAL SHAPES
Chill the sandwiches to make cutting easier. Use shaped cutters to make animals, stars, crescents or hearts as liked. Put a piece of radish on each sandwich to represent an eye or, in the case of a butterfly, a body. These would be good in lunch boxes, too.

5 Arrange a small bunch of mustard and cress or flat-leaf parsley to fit in between the sandwiches at the top. Around the base of the wigwam arrange shredded lettuce and, if liked, strips of red (bell) pepper cut zig-zag fashion along one edge. Pretzel sticks may be added to represent poles.

Smoked Salmon Pinwheels

Use a small, fresh, unsliced loaf for these so that you can cut the bread lengthways and achieve a reasonable-sized pinwheel. The bread is easier to slice if it is half-frozen.

Makes 56

1 small unsliced brown loaf
1 small lemon
75 g/3 oz/6 tbsp softened butter
15 ml/1 tbsp chopped fresh dill
225 g/8 oz smoked salmon slices
black pepper

1 Slice the loaf carefully along its length into 8 thin slices. Cut off the crusts.

2 Grate the lemon zest finely and mix together with the butter and dill.

3 Spread on each slice and arrange smoked salmon over the bread to cover, leaving a strip of buttered bread at one short end. Grind some black pepper over the top.

4 With the salmon-covered short end towards you, roll up the bread carefully and tightly, like a Swiss (jelly) roll. The buttered end will ensure the bread sticks together.

5 Wrap in clear film (plastic wrap) and chill for 1 hour. This will help the filling and bread to set in the rolled position and ensure that it does not unwind on slicing. Repeat with the remaining slices.

6 Using a sharp knife, cut each roll into 1 cm/½ in slices.

COOK'S TIP
For a tangier taste, add 15ml/1 tbsp horseradish sauce and a pinch of cayenne pepper to the butter before spreading on the bread.

Asparagus Rolls

Use green asparagus as it is usually thinner and looks more attractive. A 340 g/12 oz can usually contains about 20 spears.

2 Lay an asparagus tip at one end of the bread with the tip overlapping slightly. Roll up tightly like a Swiss (jelly) roll and press the end so that the butter sticks it together.

3 Pack the rolls tightly together, wrap in clear film (plastic wrap) and chill for 1 hour so that they set in a rolled position and do not unwind when served. Serve garnished with lemon slices and fresh flowers if liked.

Makes 20

20 slices wholemeal (wholewheat) bread,
  crusts removed
100 g/4 oz/½ cup softened butter
salt and pepper
350 g/12 oz can asparagus tips, drained
lemon slices and fresh flowers, to garnish

COOK'S TIP

Instead of spreading butter on the bread, try using the same quantity of cream cheese. Omit the salt but add ground black pepper.

1 Roll the bread lightly with a rolling pin (this makes it easier to roll up without cracking). Mix the butter and seasoning and spread over each slice of bread.

Striped Sandwiches

The bands of green, red and white of these sandwiches look very effective when displayed on a buffet table. To achieve a better contrast, add a little green food colouring to the cheese filling.

Makes 32

6 slices brown bread
4 slices white bread
1 quantity Tuna and Tomato Filling,
½ quantity Egg and Cress Filling and
½ quantity Avocado Filling (all page 20)
cucumber slices, chives and fresh flowers,
    to garnish

COOK'S TIP
These are rather fragile when cut, so wrap and chill them in the refrigerator for a couple of hours before slicing.

1 Start with a slice of brown bread and spread it with Tuna and Tomato Filling.

2 Place a white slice on top and spread with Egg and Cress Filling. Repeat with Cheese and Chive Filling, then the tuna again, using brown and white bread alternately. Repeat with the remaining fillings and bread. Wrap in foil and chill for 2 hours.

3 Unwrap, cut off the crusts and, using a sharp knife, cut into 1 cm/½ in slices. Cut the slices in half and serve garnished with cucumber slices, chives and fresh flowers if liked.

Sandwich Horns

These look very appealing for a party, but avoid using dry fillings. Smooth moist fillings, such as cream cheese, pâté or taramasalata, are suitable. Thinly sliced bread makes the shaping easier.

Makes 8

8 thin slices bread
100 g/4 oz/½ cup cottage cheese
15 ml/1 tbsp mixed chopped fresh
    parsley, chives and thyme
salt and pepper
100 g/4 oz/½ cup each Avocado
    Filling (*see* page 20) and Smoked
    Salmon Filling
few sprigs fresh herbs, to garnish

1 Remove the crusts from the bread.

2 Cut one corner off each slice, rounding it slightly. For small horns cut a smaller square of bread.

3 Mix the cottage cheese and chopped herbs together with some seasoning. Spread the bread with about half of this mixture.

4 Lift the two sides and fold one over the other with the rounded area at the base of the horn. Stick the bread in position with the filling. Secure with a cocktail stick (toothpick) and chill for 20 minutes to firm up. Repeat using the Smoked Salmon Filling and Avocado Filling.

5 Spoon the remaining filling into the horn.

6 Remove the cocktail stick before serving and garnish with a sprig of herbs.

SMOKED SALMON FILLING

Blend briefly 50 g/2 oz smoked salmon pieces in a blender with 75 ml/3 fl oz/⅓ cup double (heavy) cream, 5 ml/1 tsp lemon juice, and black pepper.

AVOCADO FILLING

Blend the flesh of 1 avocado, add 1 chopped spring onion, 10 ml/2 tsp lemon juice, a dash Worcestershire sauce, salt and pepper and blend well.

Cucumber Sandwiches

These traditional afternoon-tea sandwiches are easy to prepare and always popular. For a fresh taste, you can omit the marinade and simply use fresh sliced cucumber.

Makes 4

½ cucumber
30 ml/2 tbsp white wine vinegar
50 g/2 oz/4 tbsp softened butter
8 slices white bread
salt and pepper

1 Cut a few thin slices of cucumber to use as a garnish and set aside, then peel the rest and slice thinly. Place in a bowl, pour over the vinegar and leave to marinate for 30 minutes. Drain well.

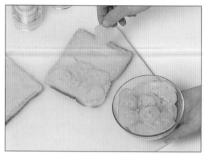

2 Butter the bread, arrange the cucumber slices over half the slices and sprinkle with salt and pepper.

3 Cover with the remaining buttered bread to make 4 sandwiches. Press together firmly and cut off the crusts. Cut each sandwich into 4 triangles and serve garnished with the cucumber slices

WATERCRESS SANDWICHES
Finely chop 1 bunch watercress. Spread 60 ml/5 tbsp mayonnaise over 8 slices buttered wholemeal (whole-wheat) bread. Arrange watercress over 4 of the slices, season and top with the other 4 slices.

Spicy Chicken Canapés

These tiny little cocktail sandwiches have a spicy filling, finished with different toppings. You can vary the ingredients: try celery and sun-dried tomatoes in place of the onions and pepper.

2 Spread the mixture over 3 of the bread slices and sandwich with the remaining bread, pressing well together. Spread the remaining Curry Mayonnaise over the top and cut into 4 cm/1½ in circles using a plain cutter.

3 Dip into paprika, chopped parsley or chopped nuts and arrange on a plate.

COOK'S TIP

Use square-shaped bread, rather than round, so that you can cut more canapé bases and have less wastage from each sandwich.

Makes 18

75 g/3 oz/⅓ cup finely chopped cooked chicken
2 spring onions (scallions), finely chopped
30 ml/2 tbsp chopped red (bell) pepper
90 ml/6 tbsp Curry Mayonnaise (*see* page 59)
6 slices white bread
15 ml/1 tbsp paprika
15 ml/1 tbsp chopped fresh parsley
30 ml/2 tbsp chopped salted peanuts

1 Mix the chicken with the spring onions and pepper and half the Curry Mayonnaise.

Index